FITRA JOURNAL:
MUSLIM HOMESCHOOLING

First Edition, 2017

Copyright 2017 Fitra Journal
www.fitrajournal.com
Editor: Brooke Benoit

Design by Reyhana Ismail
www.reyoflightdesign.com

All rights reserved. No part of this publication may be reproduced in any language, stored in any retrieval system or transmitted in any form or by any means - electronic, mechanical, photocopying, recording or otherwise - without the express permission of the copyright owner.

CONTENTS

Editorial: Brooke Benoit 4

CHAPTER 1: BEGINNINGS 7
How A Teacher Came To Homeschooling Her Children: Hafsa Abbasi 8
Embracing The Journey At Each Turn: Ilhaam al Maskery 11
Review: *7 Steps to Start Your Muslim Homeschool*: Brooke Benoit 13
Ask The Homeschoolers: Brooke Benoit and Khalida Haque 16

CHAPTER 2: THEORY, METHOD, AND STYLE 19
The Prophetic Principles of Teaching: Asma Ali 20
Three Major Mistakes Muslim Parents Make: Khalida Haque 23
Montessori Method: Importance of Freedom in Homeschooling: Ellie Fathie 25
Do Our Children Need Classic Literature? Klaudia Khan 28
Tips On Homeschooling With A Toddler In Tow: Weronika Ozpolat 30
Effective Storytelling for Young Children: Elizabeth Lymer 33
Interview: Reflections from A Well-Seasoned Journey: Chantal Blake 37

CHAPTER 3: ORGANIZING AND RETHINKING THINGS 42
Creating An Afterschool Program For Your Child: Iman Said 40
Crafting The Work-Homeschool-Life Balance: Saiyyidah Zaidi 43
Isn't Parenting About Controlling Behaviours and Outcomes? Khalida Haque 46
Finding a Blessing Where There Was Burden: Farzana Moolla Hoosen 49

CHAPTER 4: OUR FAVOURITE RESOURCES 51
Foraging - An Activity To Feed The Body And Soul: Klaudia Khan 52
Kids Learn to Stitch Review and Fun Beginning Sewing Project: Klaudia Khan 54
Favorite Storytelling Resources: Elizabeth Lymer 56
Current Favorite Resources: Asma Ali 57
Great Homeschool Bloggers: Iman Said 57
For Inspiration – Our Family's Classics Reading List: Klaudia Khan 58

Our Contributors 60

Editorial: Just Keep Showing Up

By Brooke Benoit

I am so grateful to be here today with the latest (and always greatest) issue of Fitra Journal ready to be handed over to our designer, Reyhana Ismail. For over two decades the majority of my co-workers, clients, and collaborators have been women. I know well how ridiculously over-burdened and busy we are. Add to that homeschooling and you have women who simply cannot sit down for a couple of hours and spill their thoughts onto paper. It feels like a miracle that the dozens of women who write for Fitra Journal have done just that. My appreciation runneth over, and I am assuming that many families will appreciate these journals for years to come, insha Allah. It's a blessing to see families striving in excellence, it immensely lifts me.

This issue I am also excited to share that there is a new book available for Muslim homeschoolers written by a homeschooling sister. To date I know of three such books, aside from the Fitra journals. I've written up a full review of the new book, 7 Steps to Start Your Muslim Homeschool, in Chapter 1 and listed all three titles in our Resources section.

In my own homeschooling life things have taken an odd but not unexpected turn. For many years I have wanted to open a cultural center, a place for young people to gather and receive support, to make art and foster alternative means of education. Well, I've finally done it. The first stage of the business is providing tutoring for school children and teens, which as you can imagine, is pretty weird to be in so close proximity of standardized schooling conventions, especially as my own children have never attended school. There is a lot of newness around us all at this time. But as Jameelah Madyun says in her book I mentioned, if the activities you want to do with your children don't exist, you have to create them. I wanted such a center for my family and for others. And of course none of this stuff happens over night.

My best is advice stems my favorite ayah: "Indeed, man has been created impatient and anxious." (Al-Ma'arij: 19) Slow down, listen to yourself and your children, act on what you see by adjusting what's not working while building on greater and greater things, and find support wherever you can. I hope that Fitra Journal continues to be a great support for you in your homeschooling process, thank you so much for supporting us.

Brooke Benoit, Founding Editor of *Fitra Journal* | editor@fitrajournal.com

Chapter 1
BEGINNINGS

How A Teacher Came To Homeschooling Her Children

By Hafsa Abbasi

Over a decade ago, I remember watching documentaries on television about very large families (up to fifteen children in each) sharing their lives at home. What intrigued me most was how they were homeschooled. That was one of my earliest encounters with homeschooling. A little later, after I graduated, I trained to become a primary school teacher. Even while doing so, I clearly remember thinking, *'Once I have children I would love to homeschool them'.* A short while later I got married. Fast forward to present day, I now have two beautiful young girls, one aged four and the second aged two. We live abroad in Saudi Arabia and have been doing so for the last two years. This move actually worked perfectly in my decision to homeschool, especially as I knew I wouldn't be tempted to just enroll them at state school. Also, the education cost is fairly high and some of it not to the standard we would expect. Therefore, with Allah's permission everything worked out perfectly. Alhamdulillah. So the real question is, how does it feel going from classroom teacher to homeschooling mama?

Initially, I felt nervous and just worried about my daughter's reaction to being at home all the time, and then the typical concerns about her social interactions with other children crept in. On my arrival in Saudi Arabia, when my eldest was just two years old, I set up a playgroup in my home. This helped me meet local expats, and other potential homeschooling mums too, especially as most of our children were similar ages. As the years went on and my child's needs changed, the playgroup adapted into a nursery. It will now be running as a Montessori/reception class. When Ammarah turned three – I decided to take the step – thank you to the first edition of the Fitra Journal – and made it official, publicly on my Instagram page (@mamateachesme). Then, I knew there was no turning back!

For the first week, we tried to get settled into a routine – as we would at school. I had also made a rough plan but nothing long term or with progression. I actually looked up how other homeschooling mums planned. I found some amazing tips until I saw most bought and used syllabuses catered for homeschooling to help with their child's education. At this point, I realised I need to use everything I was taught throughout my teacher training and school experience and apply it into my own homeschooling syllabus. Therefore when other mums ask me what syllabus I use, I always say I make up my own. This makes the experience of homeschooling all the more enjoyable for us. We pick and choose what we do using the resources we have available to us. This allows for our homeschooling experience to be affordable and encourages us to recycle and reuse whatever we have at home.

How I Homeschool

The way I see homeschooling is different to how I teach in some ways. For me the whole world is a classroom. Therefore we homeschool on holidays, sometimes with a plan and sometime just spontaneously. Usually though, I start by planning my themes for the year. In the past these have included themes such as: The Beach, Dinosaurs, Feelings, My Body, Healthy Eating, etc. These themes would last a week each. It was exciting for the girls and I to do it this way. This year however, our themes vary from two weeks to four weeks. I then try and plan the rest of our learning through the theme. This is very similar to what we did at school: the creative curriculum where we tried to merge all aspects of learning under one theme.

One of the most important things for me when planning is being as creative as possible. For example, one of the ways I taught my daughter to learn to write was not necessarily with pen and paper but writing in the air, tracing on my back, writing with chalk, tracing over chalk writing with a wet paintbrush, finger-painting the letter formation, and so on. My point is whenever we pencil in letter formation as an activity it has to be fun and different and something that keeps them fully engaged. Yes, this may require a little work setting up, or a bit of a hassle cleaning up, however, it is the greatest feeling ever when my child says, "Mama I want to do some learning." For me, this is a result because clearly learning is now fun and my child looks forward to it.

We link in days out with the family into our theme as well. For example, when the theme of "Under the Sea" came up one week, we scheduled a trip to the aquarium in Jeddah for an end of the week treat. Therefore, for me, going from classroom to homeschool hasn't changed entirely because the way I teach is pretty much the same, I am just less stressed about Office for Standards in Education (OFSTED), and more focused on the progress for learning.

Fitting Domestic Life Around A Busy Homeschool Life

Fitting in my household routine around homeschooling has been difficult but we have now found a way to deal with it. Our learning begins straight after breakfast for two to three hours – with play and snack breaks. By midday we begin our household cleaning, chores or cooking. At times I meal plan, but sticking to a routine does help. For my girls, the afternoon can generally be reading/looking at pictures in books, playing with Legos and basically entertaining themselves. In the winter in Saudi we look forward to more trips to the park. We hope the best for each day and celebrate the little things in life by sharing and hoping to inspire others with what we put forward for all to see. The community of homeschoolers around me and online, especially on Instagram, have been encouraging and motivating.

What's Next?

Earlier this year, I was approached by some homeschooling friends to guide them on teaching. In order to achieve this, I decided to devise a Teaching Tips course. This course was designed to help homeschooling mums be more aware of the objectives stipulated in the British National

Curriculum. This awareness, knowing what my child needs to achieve each year adds a level of confidence for the anxious homeschooling mum who may be feeling *'Is my child a little behind?'* The reality is a child receiving one-to-one attention from their teacher has more impact than a teacher's attention divided between thirty children in her class. This is the sort of information these homeschooling mums needed to hear. They just need reassurance they can do this too. You do not need to be a professional teacher to teach your children. You just need the confidence boost and some knowledge on teaching strategies especially in keeping your child engaged if that is an issue.

My current endeavours also include trying to write an easy-to-read homeschooling curriculum for Muslim homeschooling mums, including aspects of the state curriculum, Arabic, and Islamic learning. I have started to build a small bank of my tried and tested plans that I used with my daughters in order to help the homeschoolers around me and across the globe. As someone with some background in teaching I feel I have a duty to pass on this information in the best way possible in order to motivate other homeschooling mums who may initially find this route challenging.

Embracing The Journey At Each Turn

By Ilhaam al Maskery

"Everybody is a genius. But if you judge a fish by its ability to climb a tree, it will live its whole life believing that it is stupid." -Albert Einstein

Just a few weeks ago I started to develop rapidly growing concerns about the teaching-learning relationship with my children. Regardless of how much learning, bonding, and countless fun was experienced to date that momentum started to slow down. We have gotten to a stage in which my son will frown and head in the opposite direction at the thought of a "Math" or "Reading" class. The morning excitement and rush to our homeroom has decreased in spirit and at a subconscious level I sensed my son dreading the time he was about to spend learning with me, especially if it had anything to do with numbers or text. As a concerned mother-teacher my assertiveness and stubbornness to get things done anyway made me realize I was slowly transforming into a pushy information and concept feeder for the inner satisfaction that we were achieving academic outcomes. I realized that this situation completely contradicted my family's values and educational philosophies which remain the main reason for our decision to homeschool.

Upon this realization, it was time to get back on track, take a step away and reassess the situation. The thoughts that continuously surfaced to the top of my mind were: *'Why is my son rejecting the idea of math and reading in its simplest form even though I strived to deliver it through arts and games? Perhaps I wasn't striving enough. Perhaps my delivery needed a higher dose of creativity specifically catered to his personality type. Was it time for him to return to a conventional school? Perhaps my mind was neuro-linguistically programmed to a particular way of receiving education (which fortunately worked well for my learning personality) and such teaching habits were subconsciously surfacing although I was consciously exerting efforts to focus on how he learned best…'* All this was reflected through my son's reactions and responses.

I came to a realization that it simply isn't about delivering through play and arts no matter how creative it may be perceived by others. It is about delivering through play or arts which the individual learner enjoys most and that which he can relate to. It wasn't just about presenting various activities and granting him the freedom to pick his favorite, it was about presenting activities which excite him and then allow him the freedom to choose. On a few regrettable occasions I was harsh because I believed he was testing the waters for how much work he could escape and taking advantage of homeschooling. Though my harshness only came out on a few occasions it left him with an impression towards learning and enjoying certain subjects. All he needed was more motivation and activity to activate his natural child's curiosity. By now I was exploring, researching, discussing and experimenting with various approaches to reinvigorate his love-for-learning spirit. It was during this period (with sincere appreciation to the HomeSchoolers in Muscat community) that I was introduced to new ideas - simple yet functional - and became deeply inspired by the Waldorf education philosophy. I have always adopted an eclectic approach towards homeschooling and welcomed ideas from various educational philosophies and models. I believe that my son would have loved and thrived in a Waldorf setting, yet for various reasons he would not attend a Waldorf school. Instead, I brought Waldorf into my home.

I self-educated myself about the Waldorf approach by reading about it and engaging with Waldorf students, Waldorf graduates, and Waldorf teachers. I gained a deeper understanding of the approach - and the calibre and potential of students attending Waldorf Schools. Implementing some of Waldorf inspired activities at home - particularly the Four Process Story - introduced miracles in our home. My boys are singing math songs all day, subconsciously learning the fundamentals of math concepts, eager to find out what's next, and their calculating skills have progressed. I wouldn't say a major progress yet as this has all been very recent, but there are obvious signs this was a good choice for them. I am also learning as much as they are. Perhaps this week records the highest learning curve in the history of my teaching journey! The most exciting part is that my son and I are now in process of publishing a book which he plans to sell (I find it cute how he's already grasped that he can make money selling books!) Although that's not the point of this activity I will support his dream nevertheless.

Here are a few important lessons I humbly share from my own experience to encourage you to not give-up your commitment to educate your child:

• Embrace the good times as well as the challenges.

• Every child, every family, and every setting calls for a unique arrangement and learning environment.

• If you are not prepared to seek that which is best suited for your child (you know your child best) there is no guarantee that someone else will spare the time, the efforts, and the love to instill in them a love for learning.

• Become aware of different educational philosophies and learning resources.

• Capitalize on ideas which facilitate and nurture your family's educational journey, and don't completely discount a particular teaching philosophy because you disagree with some of its ideologies.

• One of the most critical reminders is to focus on the learning experience and the child instead of focusing on a check-list of grade-specific academic outcomes.

If only I had realized earlier that my son was a fish I was forcing to climb up a tree I would have taken the initiative to give him the sea to explore and resonate with. I would have also provided him with different waters to taste for different learning circumstances and subjects.

Review: *7 Steps to Start Your Muslim Homeschool*

By Brooke Benoit

I get so excited every time a Muslim homeschooler releases a book on homeschooling. I've been homeschooling for sixteen years and to date know of three such titles, not including the *Fitra Journals*. None have ever disappointed, each bringing new ideas and loads of inspiration even to an old hand like myself. Recently I thoroughly enjoyed Jameelah Madyun's new book *7 Steps to Start Your Muslim Homeschool: An Alternative to Traditional Schools*. Madyun is a former teacher and has so much experience to offer as an educator and a Muslim homeschool pioneer. I'll break it down for you chapter by chapter.

Chapter 1 Define Your Vision

This is a brilliant suggestion, one I only heard of a couple years ago even though I had known to write plenty of vision and mission statements for work purposes. I think that many of us approach homeschooling with a sense of urgency, throwing ourselves straight into the schooling part as quickly as we can and often having a tougher go of it than if we did a little warming up beforehand. I always suggest 'deschooling' a bit to readjust our attitudes about schooling, to calm down before jumping in. Now I see that deschooling along with crafting a vision statement can be an ideal way to get started. Many entrepreneurs and other leaders write vision statements for important projects, so of course doing so for homeschooling - maybe the most important thing you ever do? - is a compelling tool. If you've never done one before, no problem, Madyun offers a series of questions to guide you through the process.

Chapter 2 Plan Your Strategy

Next Madyun walks you through the major strategies or styles of homeschooling. I love her approach to this overwhelming issue, asking readers a series of questions about themselves to help access which style of home educating resonates best with them. She includes, Traditional, Unschooling, Eclectic and Charlotte Mason/Classic, then walks us through her experiences with different styles and concludes with how she currently runs her homeschooling - "a mix". I believe this may be the first time I have heard a Muslim homeschooler point out what feels obvious about the classic approach. Addressing the suggested classics and "living books" list that the style promotes she says: "It was this list that caused me to reject this approach. The majority of these books were written by Caucasian European men. There is so little diversity represented here that I didn't see a place for my African American and Muslim child. This approach is pointedly Eurocentric and frequently Christian. Although the approach itself has good points it is this over reliance on outdated western source material that I reject." Personally I find 'adapting' the classics or needing to continually 'correct' their racism, xenophobia, and often Islamophobia exhausting. While I strive to direct my children well in understanding these prevalent injustices and abuses, there are simply so many other things to do in homeschooling than correct the classics!

Through reading Madyun's further experiences you may connect to or reject some of these styles, insha Allah moving you closer to a good fit for your family with a little less firsthand discomfort. It's always reassuring to know that homeschoolers will adjust and readjust along the way, as she says: "...Although your strategy may change, your vision will remain." That vision keeps us steadfast.

Chapter 3 Gather Your Resources

"One of your biggest resources will be other homeschoolers." Yes! There is no need to do this in a vacuum, especially while homeschooling is still such a new field, with so many varied approaches and new resources coming out all the time. Listen to what has and hasn't worked for other homeschoolers. *7 Steps to Start Your Muslim Homeschool*'s book cover boasts "With over 100 resources to help get you started," and many are kindly directly linked in the e-book. Some of the suggestions are especially helpful for US families, as that is Madyun's home, but aside from all the (many free) resources she links online, others are usually easily adjustable to homeschoolers in other countries and give great inspiration to frugally go about collecting these things.

Chapter 4 Building Your Team

Team? Yes! I'm glad to see Madyun addressing outsourcing in this book, which many of us don't even consider is available to us, thinking we have to do it all as we signed up for this. She also talks straight about the fact that homeschooling is usually left entirely up to one person (the mom) and she offers suggestions for how to pull in other players. Again this is US-centric, citing things like the YMCA and the Boys & Girls Club, but you may be surprised to know that many places offer activities to children which seem school-oriented, but are available outside of a school setting, and you may just need to work a little harder to find them. While admitting, "A common complaint among many homeschoolers is that of the three main resources, often our families are the ones who are the least supportive," Madyun offers practical suggestions to to connect with and find support among our families, if possible.

She also reminds us:
As the homeschooling parent you are the core of your team. It is important that you include "self-care" as a vital part of maintaining your team. You must make sure that you take care of yourself. This means getting adequate sleep, staying healthy, keeping connected to Allah ﷻ, and taking time for yourself. (Either alone or with others.) When you are refreshed, relaxed and revitalized you will be a better teacher, guide, and a parent who will provide a better learning environment for your school.

Chapter 5 Get Organized

Madyun introduced me to a new and valuable concept that was difficult for me to initially understand: "looping." She also does a great job to explain her schedule process in a way that helps readers to let go of rigidity and see the greater picture, especially with how to combine so much running around and out-of-the house activities, which really drained me in the early years.

Chapter 6 Stay Healthy
Finally someone addresses this thing that really caught me by surprise about homeschooling, but I will leave it for you to discover when you read the book. She also offers tips for meal planning and preparing, seeking affordable and realistic physical activities for your children, and also discusses spiritual health. Madyun rightfully insists, "If you are not blessed to have organized events in your community then you will have to start them. Yes. You!" This is something I learned after many failed attempts at finding various activities. If it's not out there, you can create it. You can create co-ops, events, groups - there are so many things you will find you want to do and some things you will have to make from scratch, which is great role-modeling for our kids. Her last chapter closer addresses issues of spiritual health.

Chapter 7 Incorporate Faith
Madyun admits, "Creating a strong Islamic education in your home is not going to be easy. There are not many programs that comprise all three components equally. The three parts being Islamic values and identity, Arabic\Quran and Islamic studies." This is true, and we know that even Islamic schools aren't able to provide all of this, so that is why we homeschool. She explains some steps you can take to build a foundation for your Islamic education and to "Islamize" your studies.

A Quick Start Guide
When You need to start… now!
I hope a lot of readers come across this book either before or when they are at this stage as it is so helpful. Again, I think many of us hurl ourselves into the acts of homeschooling either because of our fears of falling behind or due to external sources pressuring us. Madyun explains, "I couldn't afford to let the kids just sit around, while I spent time researching and gathering resources. As the old proverb says; 'idle hands are the devil's workshop.'" This is the only bit I disagree with her on, as I've said before, I believe that some deschooling down time can be really beneficial to both parent and child before they embark on homeschooling. And parents could even spend that time learning about homeschooling while their kids "sit around" instead of doing what could amount to busy work. But of course few of us actually do this. So, But if you must start quickly, here is your guide! Madyun has very concisely crafted this section for you into: Quick Start Vision, Quick Start Strategy, Quick Start Team, Quick Start Resources, and Suggested Schedule - so helpful!

I absolutely adore Madyun's approach and insight into homeschooling with a Muslim point of view. I am looking forward to hearing more from her, insha Allah, starting with an interview you can find on our website. *7 Steps to Start Your Muslim Muslim Homeschool* is available as an ebook through Amazon and Barnes and Noble.

Ask The Homeschoolers

By Brooke Benoit and Khalida Haque

Thank you to everyone who sent in questions for "Ask The Homeschoolers," we hope these answers are of good use to you.

Question: Can a mom homeschool if she lacks knowledge in a particular subject area, such as sciences?
Advice: Absolutely. Firstly she probably already went through most of these courses while receiving her own education. Of course things change, new ideas are introduced, and this is one of the joys of homeschooling: we as parents have the opportunity to continue learning. Still, some subjects are going to be too daunting for some moms. I don't want to teach my children math higher than primary school level, so I use tutors for math as well as high school science subjects and languages other than English. You don't have to do it all.

And you can always learn something alongside your child(ren) if you didn't get the chance to learn it during your own education. It will show your child(ren) that you are never too old to learn and that learning is a lifelong practice.

Question: Can a mom homeschool if she has mental health challenges/issues?
Advice: That's something only she can decide for herself and it is very dependent upon the severity of her challenges/issues and how (frequently and for how long) they impact her. It is important not be pressured into anything that doesn't feel feasible or right. And it is also essential that if she cannot homeschool to be able to not see herself lacking in any way for it. Not everyone is meant to homeschool or to be homeschooled. I would suggest praying, of course, and at the same time exploring with a counsellor or psychotherapist her concerns and how she might proceed to homeschool if that is what she wants to do. With the help of her therapist she can create plans that will enable her to manage her condition and her children's schooling. Within her schedules she can make provisions for times when she feels that she isn't doing so well psychologically and needs to step back. She can even weave in an exit strategy that she can refer to if she decides not to continue.

Some countries have flexi-schooling whereby children can attend school part-time, however from my understanding this is through negotiation with the individual school and the principal/headteacher. If she feels up to homeschooling she can go for it. She needs to maintain everything she can to take care of herself as she does so. It is paramount that she be willing to seek help when she needs it or to teach other adults who regularly interact with her and her family the signs of when she may be slipping and in need of help. If she's a single mother then she will need to teach these to her children and to whom to turn to if they spot them happening. And please accept the assistance when it is offered.

Question: Where do you find inexpensive resources besides the library?
Advice: One of the great things about having a tight budget to homeschool is that it can really help you to narrow down what are the most important things. Be sure to discuss these things with your children to gauge what things are most important to them too, this is a good way to help them prioritize and respect money.

There are loads of free resources online, the book I reviewed for this issue, *7 Steps to Start Muslim Homeschooling*, lists many good ones. Used items are also helpful, in addition to second hand shops there are places such as resell shops and flea markets ("souks" where I live); homeschooling, parenting or other resell groups on Facebook and other social media; as well as listings for desirable items in local papers and online resell websites.

Question: How do I homeschool with a range of ages - especially with a newborn and toddler in the mix?
Advice: Weronika Ozpolat has written about homeschooling with a toddler in chapter two, but mixing a newborn into the family... The first thing is to allow the entire family to enjoy this brief time with the newborn, our children's relationships are an important aspect of homeschooling. I have seven children and during this precious time I remind them to remain flexible, when the baby sleeps or is otherwise preoccupied then we will do something that requires my attention, otherwise they can do many things on their own or with occasional assistance. They definitely take advantage a bit as kids do. Be sure to encourage a lot of independence at this point, they should be able to get their activities and selves ready for your time together, not waiting on you to do things they can easily do themselves, such as gathering materials or getting ready to go out. Don't worry too much about this time, there are lots of large homeschooling families who have experienced this over and over, it passes too quickly and insha Allah you can then make up any time you feel was lost (but it wasn't!).

Question: My big one is, how do I fit in home education around housework and other chores/duties? And will I be able to do enough for them and give them an enriching education experience? I have a lot of self-doubt.
Advice: For me, letting go of needing a showroom-perfect house is necessary to be a homeschooler. There are many other things I rather do than keep my home immaculate and serve elaborate meals. And those other things are exactly the things that are enriching and make homeschooling so interesting for both children and parents. As kids get older they can and should help a lot, especially with food preparation and cooking. These are life skills not taught in school, but something homeschoolers often do well.

For you it's helpful to develop some larger organizing schemes, such as menu planning and bulk shopping, as well as seasonal activities like going through wardrobes, toys and so on. It's also important to let the other parent know what all you do so they can understand what is happening instead of what they may see not be happening. When you have self-doubt, it's good to look to your support network - look to other homeschoolers, our houses are messy, but we are doing great things and our kids appreciate it.

Question: What if your kids want to go to school? How do you explain why you're not sending them?
Advice: With seven children, I've gone through this a few times. My response varies according to the age of the curious. For older kids I tell them that they will have to commit to at least six months. It's a lot of work to organize their home education and then also work to prepare and enroll them in school, so they need to be ready to give it a real solid chance if they truly want to try it. None of them have yet to commit, but that's what I ask for when the older ones say they want to. For the younger ones, I usually just explain that they'll have to get up really early to catch the bus. It's really just a variation of my first argument and they stop pining for it within less than a week of missing the bus everyday!

I also explain to them that school looks like fun, all those kids trotting off to do it every morning makes it look to our kids like a big party, but it's not. My kids have talked to other kids about their experiences and that alone is off-putting. But I also tell them that I know I can provide a better education and avoid all the pain that comes along with going to school.

Question: How can we homeschool, insha Allah, with two full-time working parents?
Advice: Saiyyidah Zaidi shares her family's unique story in chapter three and is worth a read for another point of view. I initially worked full-time from home when we began homeschooling, my husband watched the kids while I worked in the early mornings. Later I worked in our family owned business during the hours my husband was home with the kids and vice versa. I burnt out very quickly in this lifestyle as I felt that the homeschooling was dumped in my lap in addition to my workload. He didn't do any directly homeschooling activities with the kids. I regret abruptly leaving my job instead of trying harder to communicate with my spouse or at least giving him two weeks notice.

If you're going to both share the weight of contributing to the family finances, then obviously you'll need to share the load of all the domestic duties too, including homeschooling. This will take a lot of communication and planning. It's rare, but if both parents commit and put in the effort it can work.

Chapter 2
THEORY, METHOD, AND STYLE

The Prophetic Principles of Teaching

By Asma Ali

If you were to ask me what my favorite memory of homeschooling has been thus far, I'd have to say it's linked to a feeling: the immense pride, satisfaction, and plain happiness I felt watching my children read and write, knowing that I taught them how to do that. With my first son, I remember trying to pick the best books to help me teach, buying flashcards and aids, and it all working great - only for none of it to work with my second son! In fact, hardly any of the material I accumulated for various subjects (and there was a ton of it – new homeschoolers be warned: stop buying everything you see!) seemed to make a difference. So, I started asking questions: *Is he just not ready to learn? Does he not like the material or is it the way I teach? What can I do or change to help productive learning?* I didn't know it at the time, but all these questions were related to an important aspect in education: teaching methodology.

What Is Teaching Methodology?

Simply put, it's the method or style of teaching we use to explain information in order to achieve learning outcomes. What we're teaching is obviously important, but it's easy to forget that the way we teach is just as – if not more – crucial. We only have to look to our own Islamic heritage to find just how rich it is with teaching principles and methods, and there is no better teacher and role model to take from than the prophet Muhammad ﷺ himself.

Can you remember your favourite teacher? Chances are they had a warm personality, an interest in their students, and a knack for motivation. Good teachers are amongst the few people in our childhoods who can have such a great impact in our lives and, as homeschooling parents, we have a unique opportunity to be the ones who inspire and encourage our children in their education – Islamic and otherwise. The Prophet ﷺ defined the role of a teacher as a 'connector' first as he was enthusiastic and engaged in the lives of those around him. By understanding the techniques and principles used by the Prophet ﷺ and implementing them in our own homeschool routines, we can embody the characteristics of the best teacher, improve our own methods, and ensure we are teaching effectively.

Eight Principles The Prophet ﷺ Used To Teach The Companions

The following is not an exhaustive list, but some of the main ways the Prophet ﷺ taught the companions, based on my notes from the course 'Teaching Methodology" by Imtiyaz DaMiel at Knowledge International University (shared with his permission).

1. Establish a motive for learning

A key to the amount of effort we put into any activity is motivation. The Prophet ﷺ achieved this in two ways: a) pointing out the benefits and virtue of learning, and b) creating a desire to learn. The merit of learning in Islam is mentioned throughout the Qur'an and sunnah. The Prophet ﷺ said, "Whoever follows a path seeking knowledge, Allah will make the path to paradise easy." *(Bukhari)* But this doesn't mean all learning is restricted to the deen. Regularly remind your children and explain the advantages of studying both their religion and other subjects as we are taught to pray for success in this life and the next.

2. Encourage and praise the child

Praising our children when they work hard and do something right is a great way to enforce positive behavior. The Prophet ﷺ often praised the companions for their knowledge and encouraged them to ask him questions. This type of encouragement is a powerful tool for us in creating an open atmosphere at home where our children feel comfortable and free to discuss not only work, but also whatever is on their mind.

3. Know the abilities and mental capacity of your children

One of the best things about homeschooling is being able to tune into the way your child learns best and what they have a natural aptitude for. Not everyone is born to be a doctor or academic and our job is to develop the skills our children already possess and guide them. In the seerah, we learn about the different strengths of the companions and how they used them to leave their own mark in society – some memorized the Qur'an, others were good at trade whilst some became jurists. Find your child's passion and natural talent and help them excel.

4. Take individual differences into consideration

In one narration, the Prophet ﷺ was in the middle of giving a khutbah when a man came in and said, "Messenger of Allah, here is a person who has no knowledge about his religion." The Prophet interrupted his khutbah, asked for a chair to be brought to him and taught the man certain things before resuming. *(Bukhari)* All children have different needs that ought to be prioritized. I am now trying to get my boys to study together, but am aware that one needs a different level of attention and tailoring lessons to his individual learning style has worked wonders. Don't forget to take your time in covering the basics before moving on to something your child just isn't ready for.

5. Guide students to their appropriate field

An extension of point three, it is also worth reading and contemplating on the advice of Ibn al Qayyim:

"One of the things that should be done is to consider the nature of the child and what he is capable of doing and has a potential for. If it is then discovered that he has the potential of doing a certain type of job, you should not force him to do something else. If a parent forces his child to pursue something for which the boy has no interest, the boy will not do well and will miss what he has the potential of being good at."

6. Make learning exciting!

The more a student is engaged, the better the learning will be. Ibn Mas'ood narrated: "The Prophet used to choose the right time of the day to preach to us, lest we got bored." *(Bukhari)* And this is a really important point – know when to engage your children for the best results. We all know what a battle it is to teach when our kids are preoccupied with other thoughts, so make good use of morning hours when they are more alert. Make use of good weather and enjoy a lesson outdoors. Also, one of the most common ways to teach involves lecturing and looking at a book, but we need to start thinking outside the box to keep up the interest. For younger children, try not to rely so much on worksheets, introduce more play.

7. Use a variety of methods to explain a point

Did you know that when we look at a picture, the brain stores the information we see for a longer period of time than if it was just written? Using different methods to convey information means the retention of learning is much greater. The Prophet ﷺ would keep his teaching interesting and fresh by making illustrations in the sand, posing questions to arouse curiosity, making analogies, using gestures, and telling stories. Get creative and switch up the way you teach to make it fun and maximize learning!

8. Teach an objective approach

Teaching objectivity creates critical thinkers. We are living in an era where our children have access to all sorts of information at their fingertips and are exposed to a variety of viewpoints. Objectivity enables them to analyse different types of information and follow a correct understanding. The Prophet ﷺ used several methods to develop the characteristic of objectivity, including explained reasoning, discussion and review, and looking at two sides of an argument. He also trained the sahaba to deduce answers as the ability to evaluate and judge information is the highest level of thinking and the Prophet ﷺ encouraged it.

By applying all these principles in his teaching, the Prophet ﷺ cultivated great personalities and people who would change the world around them. As much as my homeschooling journey is already filled with fond memories for myself, I want it to be a time that is memorable, for all the right reasons, for my children too. This is our opportunity to move away from education as institutional learning and nurture our children with love and respect, creating lifelong learners whilst following the footsteps of our beloved Prophet ﷺ.

Three Major Mistakes Muslim Parents Make

By Khalida Haque

Before we become parents, I don't think we really consider how we are going to do it, how we are going to parent. It's more often than not an assumption that we will just know how to. Rarely do we consider the pitfalls and plan on how to manage them. It is once we are parents, and usually when the problems arise, that we research how to overcome them. Or we muddle through somehow. Here are three common mistakes that we as Muslim parents tend to make and how we might resolve them.

We Forget That Our Children Are Not Ours

We believe that our children belong to us. Which means that we see them as extensions of ourselves rather than what they truly are, which is an amanah (trust, gift) from Allah. And that they are a part of the testing we will encounter in this world:

"And know that your properties and your children are but a trial and that Allah has with Him a great reward." (Al Anfal: 28)

"Your wealth and your children are but a trial, and Allah has with Him a great reward." (At Taghabun: 15)

When we forget that they are not really ours we try to control them as we would if something were a part of us. We see them as part of our reputation and believe, depending upon what they do and how they behave, others will see us as good or bad. The effort and struggle to parent well is ours but the outcome is not.

Solution:

Recognise that your child is an individual that Allah has created and handed to you to rear. Keep in mind this quote by Angela Schwindt, a homeschooling mom: "While we try to teach our children all about life, our children teach us what life is all about." Which reminds us that we may parent our children but Allah has granted our children to us to teach us something we would otherwise not be able to learn.

We Assume We Know Them

This assumption means that we do not then spend time getting to know them. And when they don't behave in the way we think they ought to be we become lost: *'How did this happen? This is not my child! ...'* If we make parenting mistake #1 and believe that they are an extension of ourselves we almost always then fall into this mistake too.

Solution:
See that your children are separate beings. They are not you. They are not their siblings. Or anyone else. They are their own selves. Perfectly created: *"We have indeed created man in the best of moulds."* (At Teen: 4). Take the time to get to know them. Spend time with them. Play with them. Have conversations with them. As they grow, let them take on responsibilities appropriate to their age. Watch and observe them in wonder. Reflect upon how they have grown and matured.

We Try To Make Them What We Want Them To Be
Due to mistakes #1 and #2 we try to make them into what they are often not. Or we try to live through them because we feel unfulfilled in some way or other and we have regrets at perhaps not achieving what we think we were capable of.

"In the absence of reflection, history often repeats itself…Research has clearly demonstrated that our children's attachment to us will be influenced by what happened to us when we were young if we do not come to process and understand those experiences."
~Dan Siegel

As parents it is not our role to make our children into something. We are here to facilitate their journey into becoming who they are, who they are meant to be. And they are here to help us recognise what we contain within ourselves so that we may address it and harness it. We need to heal and they need to grow.

Solution:
Do the work to heal yourself and insha'Allah the rest will fall into place. Take an interest in your child, as Peter Jackson has explained: "It's one thing to support your kid, but if you have an interest in what your child is doing, it makes it a whole lot easier." I have noticed a lot of adults who were moulded by parents into what they want - usually lawyers, doctors, or similar - have returned to childhood dreams of being artists or beauticians or writers. Or they failed to conform initially. We cannot make people into who they are not. And accepting our child for who they are makes life so much easier. Helping them figure that out can be a lot of fun and create beautiful memories.

If we can avoid or remedy these three mistakes in our parenting we will, bi'idhnillah, have strong resilient children and there will be less broken adults that require repair, insha'Allah:

"It is easier to build strong children than to repair broken men."
~Frederick Douglass

Montessori Method:
Importance of Freedom in Homeschooling

By Ellie Fathie

'Whatever an education is, it should make you a unique individual, not a conformist; it should furnish you with an original spirit with which to tackle the big challenges; it should allow you to find values which will be your road map through life; it should make you spiritually rich, a person who loves whatever you are doing; wherever you are, whomever you are with; it should teach you how to live and how to die."
Dumbing Us Down *by John Taylor Gatto*

Whenever I think of how I want the education in my home to be, this quote always springs to mind. This image Gatto depicts gives me energy to carry on home educating my children everyday as it encapsulates every aspect of their lives and takes me to the bigger picture of their education, not merely their academic education. However, sometimes I'm left with the question, *but how?* How can I enable my children to achieve this type of education? Which way do I follow and how can this be practically applied in the home?

The answer to that question was gifted to me during one cold December night when I was reading for an assignment I had for my Montessori teacher diploma. I was reading one of Maria Montessori's books and realised that the way to achieve this type of education is through freedom and freedom alone. We see that the traditional schooling system is all about controlling the children and forcing them to learn things they did not choose at a time they did not choose, and in a style they did not particularly want or choose. A lot of home educators choose to take it upon themselves to gain back that control and give the children back their power of choice.

Many of us choose to homeschool because we value and respect children's ability to follow their passion and interests. We want to nurture their curiosity and love for learning. We don't want them to be judged by someone else's standards or conform to someone else's idea of what should or shouldn't be. In a nutshell home education is a form of freedom of its own. I will shed more light in this article on the importance of freedom and how we can apply it in our home education environment following some key principles from the Montessori method.

To apply freedom in our home education we first have to bear in mind the link between freedom and the following concepts:

Freedom and Independence

In her book *Education and Peace*, Maria Montessori said "Without freedom it is impossible for personality to develop fully. Freedom is the key to the entire process, and the first step comes when the individual is capable of acting without help from others and becomes aware of himself as an autonomous being." Therefore, in order for child to be free, he/she needs first to become independent. Hence, the main focus in the first six years of my children's life is on helping them achieve independence in their day to day life skills: to be able to accomplish everyday tasks on their own without having to ask for help from adults, and to enable them to take care of their own personal needs. Supporting children towards more independence and enabling them to look after their basic needs gives them confidence and helps them gain the varied experiences needed to become fully functioning adults.

Freedom in A Prepared Environment

The phrase "prepared environment" refers to a well-thought out environment, designed with the child in mind. The goal of the prepared environment is to foster independence and allows the child to have the freedom to explore. There are activities laid on the shelves beautifully and in an orderly manner that are developmentally appropriate, there is a control of error mechanism where the child can easily correct him/herself and also bear a level of challenge for the child to hold his/her concentration long enough to help him/her learn from those activities and gain new concepts.

Freedom of Movement and Choice

The children in this prepared environment are free to choose any activity from the shelves as soon as they have been given a lesson on it or they can ask for a lesson if the activity looks interesting to them. They are free to move, to take the activity and work with it on a table or on the floor. They are free to choose as long as they don't harm themselves, others or destroy the materials they are working with, apart from that they have the freedom to choose anything from the carefully and purposely prepared environment.

As the child grows he/she is given more responsibility towards his/her education. Children between ages of three to six are generally free to choose any activity from the shelves, and since the activities are well thought out and serve a purpose any choice they make will scaffold their learning experiences. However, once the child moves from the early years stage and starts the elementary stage at six he/she is expected to have accountability for his/her learning.

For example, my six year-old daughter has to work on a few subjects on a daily basis so if she has a note from me in her book that she needs to work on multiplication on a certain day she may choose to work using any of the multiplication materials on the shelf wither with beads, multiplication table, or use the charts. She is also expected to self-correct and then comes to check her work with me at the end which gives her ownership over her learning experience and gives her confidence over her own abilities. Having said that, it does not mean she is just left to her own devices, I observe her and gently guide her and offer activities that either she doesn't show much interest in or show her how to deal with concepts she might be struggling with.

Freedom Within Limits

The freedom of choice is dependent on the prepared environment and dependant on certain rules of conduct agreed upon, such as not harming oneself, others, or the materials, as well as taking only one activity off the shelf at a time and ensuring it is returned back to the shelf in full, working order so it's ready for another child to use it.

Hence the freedom in our home education environment is what Montessori called "freedom within limits". These limits are explained to the children, role played often, and practiced from a young age. The children thrive in an orderly environment where they know what to expect. These limits are also common sense that portray respect for each other and our environment.

Maria Montessori has written about freedom of choice extensively, making a powerful argument that the roots of tyranny we see in the world around us result from adults forcing children to obey their commands. When a child spends his/her time everyday following the instructions of adults and has no right to follow their own interests, they may start to believe their own interests are of no importance. He/she then will lose confidence in his/her abilities and start to believe that their thoughts are not as important as the thoughts of the adults who are teaching him/her or those who hold a place of authority or are superior over them.

Freedom does not contradict discipline, but the way to reach discipline is by creating environments where children can find engaging materials to use and naturally they will get curious. Moreover, to ensure child's engagement with the materials and cultivate the love to work takes time, patience, and practise. However, once the child is fully engaged in the work that appeals to him/her at their particular level of development, they become self-disciplined and then freedom of choice becomes a habit of mind which opens the floodgates to creativity.

We aspire for our children to be responsible, free thinking adults and whether homeschooled or not we all need limits to keep us secure and safe, limits also guide our relationships with one another and help us better understand and value freedom. Allah has honoured human beings by the freedom of choice: "There shall be no compulsion in [acceptance of] the religion. The right course has become clear from the wrong. So whoever disbelieves in Taghut and believes in Allah has grasped the most trustworthy handhold with no break in it. And Allah is Hearing and Knowing." (Al-Baqarah: 256) However, once the choice is made there are consequences and responsibilities that come with that choice. As Muslims we are expected to follow Allah's orders once we accept Islam, to pray in a certain way, fast in a certain manner, and so on.

Freedom of choice is the first introduction to responsibility, while choices give the child freedom we also help him/her develop problem solving and decision making which they need to survive in life. Choices also foster in the child resilience as he /she takes a responsibility, enables him/her to take an action then bear the consequences of this particular action. This in turn helps pave the way for the Islamic cultivation of the child as being a true believer, being responsible for their own actions and choices. Moreover, freedom of choices gives the child confidence, encourages independence, and eliminates power struggles between the parents and the children - something that can be detrimental to the parent-child connection, especially in the homeschool environment.

Do Our Children Need Classic Literature?

By Klaudia Khan

I once attended an interesting lecture about children's education by Zohra Sarwari, an author, speaker, and homeschooling mother from the United States. Sarwari is a great speaker, she had me making notes all throughout her speech. But there was one point in particular that got me thinking: she said that she wouldn't let her children read Shakespeare as she didn't see any good in a story of two lovers who disobey their families and commit suicide. There is much more to Shakespeare than *Romeo and Juliet*, but examining it through the lenses of an Islamic worldview, is it really that good? Is it relevant for me? Should my children read it?

In my search for the answer I came across a blog by Elizabeth Y. Hanson, homeschooling educator and author of a curriculum based on classics. Hanson is also a Muslim, so it was interesting to read on her page: "...if your children grow up reading classic literature, they will always be able to read difficult literature, and all doors to great literature and knowledge will be open to them. Not to mention that they will be able to think, speak, and write at higher levels, too. Reading the classics also trains us in understanding human nature; why people do the things they do and how to recognize the good person from the bad person, to put it simply. Shakespeare was the all-time master of this."

So, is Shakespeare good or not? I want my children to learn to appreciate "good" literature, but I also want to make sure that the content is good. I know that expecting pure halal content compatible with Islamic values and culture is perhaps too much to ask from popular classics, but how then to define their worth for our children? How to define 'good'?

The Islamic School League of America might help here with their classified list of "Books Recommended for Islamic Values and Excellent Writing". The list, prepared by author and educator Dr. Freda Crane Shamma, suggests popular children classics with ratings based on quality, enjoyment, and Islamic values. "There are many thousands of books aimed at young people, and thousands of them are appealing to children. In preparing this list of books that develops and/or reinforces Islamic values, we are not suggesting that children should not read any of the appealing 'fluff', those books that entertain but don't teach," writes Dr. Shamma on the ISLA website.

And if the book you have in mind for your child is not included in the list you can assess its suitability using Dr. Shamma's criteria:

1. Family is important (rather than emphasis on individualism).

2. Family is comprised of humans (rather than dogs or other pets).

3. Best friends should be of the same gender (for older children).

4. Witches and magic have a minor role (preferably firmly placed in a fantasy world).

5. Working for the good of others is important.
(Source: https://theisla.org/instructional-resources/the-reading-list/#link_tab-learn)

So I am happy to learn that there are classic books suitable for Muslim children. Just which ones to choose? I search for "must-read classics" and "world classics" and the results come as another surprise. Most of the titles on every list are classics of English literature. Even if it's a world classics list there are only a handful of French or Russian titles, few American ones, and the majority is English British literature. Classic novels are considered "difficult" even by mainstream readers, and what about Muslim children who might feel unrepresented as well as unbothered by the old books? Because my children are Muslim, but also Polish and Pashto, as well as British for being born and raised in the UK, I want them to learn to appreciate the heritage of each of these cultures. It's no problem finding English or Polish classic books, even considering the condition of Muslim suitable content. But finding the classics of Pashto literature is more tricky, as the culture of Pashtuns is based on oral tradition rather than written. And when it comes to the literature of other Muslim countries, in Arabic and other languages, you find that not many classics are translated into English and of what there is not much might be appropriate for young readers. The only book that stands as representation of classic Arabic literature is the *1001 Nights*.

Compiling a classic literature list for our children might be tricky, but not impossible, especially with such tools as Dr. Shamma's criteria of content quality. Looking through the popular classics list is a good starting point, but I firmly believe that your family library should reflect your heritage, and so there is no one-size-fits-all book list that would suit everyone, just as there is not one education model to fit everyone. But we know it already, we are homeschoolers.

Klaudia shares her family's favorite classic literature titles on page 58 of this edition of Fitra Journal.

Tips On Homeschooling With A Toddler In Tow

By Weronika Ozpolat

When I tell people that I homeschool my children, I am often asked how I manage it. I have three children, and one on the way, so I have to juggle multiple age groups with different needs. People often think this must be challenging and one of the biggest things they want to know is how I can possibly homeschool with younger children around. Do they cause too many distractions? How can I keep them occupied? How can we get anything done?

Well, it is not as hard as you may think. I see homeschooling as a family affair. We do as much as we can together and I always try to include my youngest in what we are doing. In fact, he often wants to be involved. Here are some of my best tips on how to homeschool with a toddler around. With some simple strategies, you can do it too.

Get your toddler involved

When you are homeschooling multiple age groups, you become an expert at adapting the task to suit each child. After all, it is much easier to work together than arrange completely different activities for each child. For example, while working on our star topic, the children drew the sun on some black paper using chalk pastels. After they had drawn the picture, my eldest wrote facts about the sun around her picture, my middle child cut out the facts and stuck them around his picture and my toddler was quite happy drawing on a piece of paper and then cutting up another sheet of paper. We were all at the same table, working on the same thing, but each child experienced the task differently according to their abilities.

Each time you plan a task, ask yourself how you can step this task up for an older child and how you can step it down for a younger child. It may seem difficult at first but you will soon get used to thinking of ways to adapt each activity to suit different members of your family.

Set up a separate activity for your toddler

If the task cannot be adapted for your toddler, you can set up a separate activity for them. Always set up this activity in the same room you are working with your other children in. This way, you are available to help either your toddler or your school age children, whichever needs help at the time.

Good activities for toddlers at this time could be:

Play Dough
This is always a fun activity for children and can hold their interest for long periods of time as they explore it in different ways. Give your toddler some cookie cutters and a rolling pin or give them cupcake cases and ask them to make some cakes. Give them some small parts such as buttons or pebbles to press into the playdough; of course make sure you have your eye on them if they are at the age where they put everything into their mouth. Give them some animal figures and they can do some imaginative play. Give them sticks to push into the play dough or cut it up with butter knives. There are so many possibilities.

Construction Toys
These have to be one of my favourite toys for children. They are great for developing fine motor skills as well as hand eye coordination. They develop imagination and creativity which can lead to improved problem-solving skills. They have also been shown to boost mathematical skills and improve spatial awareness. Children learn so many skills through this kind of play with very little effort from us. These kinds of learning experiences make the life of a homeschooling parent easy! Construction toys such as building blocks, Duplo, and Magna-Tiles can offer toddlers endless fun while they acquire so many skills.

Water Play
Most toddlers love to play with water and my toddler is no exception. Give him a tub of water and some cups and these will keep him occupied for a long period of time. Like construction toys, water play provides children with many learning opportunities. It allows them to develop problem solving skills as they figure out the properties of water. Which things float and which things sink? What happens when you pour water through a sieve? What happens when you fill up a container and pour it out? Toddlers can discover the answers to these questions, and many others, through water play. Keep in mind that small children can drown in very little water, always be in the same room with your child when they play with water.

Sensory Play
This is another type of play particularly loved by toddlers. Sensory play stimulates the senses which, in turn, stimulates neural pathways in the brain boosting brain development. Set up a sensory tub filled with dried beans or oats or sand. Throw in some animal figures, utensils, cardboard tubes or whatever you fancy. By exploring these objects toddlers are able to learn all about the world around them.

Homeschool During Naptime
If your toddler still has a daily nap, as most toddlers do, this can be a great time for you to get the bulk of your homeschooling done. Whether this works for you will probably depend on the time your toddler usually takes a nap each day and whether this coincides with your homeschooling time. We do the bulk of our learning in the morning, however, my toddler takes a nap around midday so he is usually with us during school time. If you can manage to tie in your learning time with your toddler napping, things will probably be a lot easier for you!

Educational Activities

The play activities I have already mentioned offer so many learning experiences for your toddler, however, you can also set up separate educational activities for them too but make sure the activity is appropriate for their age group. There should be no pressure for them to formally learn at this age but a lot of toddlers may enjoy fun activities with an educational undertone. Here are some ideas:

Sorting
Get a segmented dish or a few different dishes. Then give your toddler some small objects to sort, for example, pattern blocks, animals, cereal, coloured dice or coloured stones. Leave them to sort the pile of objects into the different bowls or compartments of the segmented dish.

Match the object to the flashcard
Get some flashcards and objects that match the objects on the flashcards. Let your toddler place the objects on the correct flashcards.

Mark making
Fill a tray with salt or sand and give your toddler a stick. Let them use the stick to make marks in the salt or sand. They could also use their fingers for this instead of a stick. Show them how to make zig zags, shapes or swirls. This is a great activity that is a precursor for handwriting later on.

Little helper
If your toddler is anything like mine, they will love to help you around the house. Give them a dustpan and brush, a sponge to wash some dishes, or let them help you prepare food. Toddlers enjoy being involved in what we are doing. Not only do they enjoy spending time with us, they love to imitate what we are doing. Imitation is their way of learning about the world they live in. Everything is fun for them at that age, even chores, so make the most of their enthusiasm while it lasts!

Books
If your older children can be left to complete something on their own, why not take the chance to read some books to your toddler. Reading to your child is an excellent way to instil a love of reading in them and it is important to do this at a young age. Research shows that reading to babies and young children improves literacy outcomes in later life.

I hope this article has given you some ideas of what you can do with your toddler while your older children are doing their school work. With a little thought and practise you will be able to manage multiple age groups in your homeschool with ease.

Effective Storytelling for Young Children

By Elizabeth Lymer

Why

As a children's fiction writer and family storyteller, I believe in the educational value of stories to such a great extent that – alongside free play – I have relied upon stories as my primary tool for informal home learning in the early years. My eldest child is currently nine. In him and all my children, alhamdulillah, I have witnessed strengths in solution-finding, strategic thinking, creativity, imagination, exploration, experimentation, articulation, dialogue, expression, and strong storytelling in fantasy play which I attribute to engagement with stories. Allah ﷻ knows best.

In the Qur'an, Allah ﷻ invites us to tell stories and parables. He directs us to particular ones but He does not limit us to those. We know that Muhammad ﷺ was an exceptionally good listener when people told him of their trials in the hopes he would help them make changes in the best direction for good ends. Also, Isa عليه السلام communicated a lot of his message through stories, and he is the only prophet who will return to help humans before the end of the world.

Following Isa's عليه السلام example, we can be inspired to use stories for guidance and healing. We can strive to be storytellers and good communicators, and to raise children who will be well equipped to join Isa عليه السلام in his mission for the sake of Allah ﷻ, when he arrives, insha Allah. However, we have to be careful. In the conflicting histories of Isa's عليه السلام death, we can deduce a warning of the danger of mistaking fabricated stories for true ones. We don't want to mislead or to lie when we tell stories – or when perform any of our deeds.

I recommend interactive storytelling to include, engage, and nurture listeners as storytellers themselves. If we let our listeners tell stories with us – putting into play intentions, ideas, hopes – we can gently facilitate them to tell stories on their own, to structure intentional, persevering, strong, successful stories for themselves in their lives, insha Allah.

What

I like to rely upon established story plots/structures in creating new stories and to choose old stories to tell or retell. (And this was the way of Shakespeare and is the way of Julia Donaldson, author of Gruffalo and many other children's books.) This protects me from making the mistake of relaying useless narrative. When using fiction, I omit details from stories that conflict with Islam, or I include them yet talk about them, guiding my children to notice and class them as make-believe or beliefs belonging to a different creed. I want my children to develop skills in identifying untruth, and I find fictional stories to be a safe place for learning them.

I am aware that some Muslim parents consider fictional stories as worse than useless: detrimental. I think this is only the case if they are presented untruthfully as factual. When children witness me making up a story about them as the main characters, and they contribute to it, they are aware it is fiction. In as much as they are capable of separating their dreams, desires, and actual activity at their stage of development; for instance, when asked simply, "What did you do today?" some three, four, and five year olds relate memories that mix imagination with reality because they embrace their creative minds as much as their sensory experiences, and do not need to sort and separate them.

We can help children to establish boundaries between pretend, made up stories, and real-life, non-fiction by having dialogue about these differences when the child is ready. I have taken my cues from my children when they have started asking, "Is that possible?" and, "Did that really happen?" I have found they often don't care for clarity regarding fiction and non-fiction until about six years old, and I don't mind as long as they care about the absolute awesomeness of Allah ﷻ.

How

To actively connect with listeners, I like to make my storytelling interactive. At home, my young children and I have enjoyed going on 'voyage and return' journeys, wherein we lead characters – often bearing the children's own names – through various choices, discoveries, and achievements before returning them home. I lead the story and we improvise our plot in a safe story structure for creativity.

I don't want to waste time or mislead anyone with empty narrative. For example, a day in the life of a character who gets everything they want is just a series of events with no contrast between the beginning, middle, and end. For this reason, I often use and recommend using the good old structure of a 'quest' to guide interactive, improvised storytelling.

Start with the main character(s) doing something they like or are good at, introduce what they want, drive the story by putting obstacles in their way, and show the character(s) overcoming them. During the middle of the story, show character(s) try, try, and try again to find what they are searching for, or achieve their goal. (Give them three obstacles before you let them succeed.) To conclude the story, have the main character(s) do what they set out to do by using skills acquired through the activity they were shown doing at the story outset. End the story with their success and show them living in some sort of contrast to how they began – or show them learning/benefitting from their failures, and discovering wisdom/experience of greater value than what they had sought.

"After salat, she decided to go out because she wanted…." "He made du'a and then he announced his decision to…." "Remembering that Allah always gives her everything she needs, she used her favourite umbrella she'd brought with her to…." "He thought back over the changes he had been through that day, and especially thanked Allah for…." Masha'Allah, children soon understand the rhythm of participation and often build a joyful momentum as they contribute to the direction of the story with intentions, decisions, actions, and reflections.

I like to show my children that I have noticed their current interests, talents, and abilities by including their favourite activities in the initial scene, and referring to their interactive inputs in the process of developing and describing the story world. With four children to facilitate, I find this a great short term memory work out, subhanAllah. And it encourages my children to value their interests and see potential in their developing skills. Also, we all find it fun and memorable, alhamdulillah.

As you can see from my above examples to invite interaction, it is easy to make improvised storytelling Allah-centred.

When

Do I engage my children with interactive or simply oral storytelling everyday? No. Yesterday, I read from my favourite storytelling book*, along with a couple of Beatrix Potter tales. But the day before I neither read nor told my children one story – they only engaged independently through audiobooks. Today we listened to stories in the car and tonight we created an interactive story using the model above – alhamdulillah. Some days I don't think they engage with any stories, and I'm not comfortable with that – but I have to remember we talk a lot, telling one another stories of our personal news all the time, discussing stories we're reflecting upon, and making the stories of our lives.

I knew from the outset of parenting I would not be able to be strictly routined. It's not who I am. And I am not a perfectionist. When training in oral storytelling, I learned that is is more powerful to tell a story from the heart, eye to eye, than to read it from a book, with several glances to listeners. But I prefer to opt for dramatic or gentle reading rather than to never get around to having a storytelling experience at all. I know that my children experience joy from interactive storytelling, usually open up about all kinds of thoughts afterwards, and often sleep soundly. But I prefer to let it go if it is past bedtime and I haven't started to share or create something.

Also, I value read-aloud stories as much as storytelling, masha'Allah. I use books more that memory and imagination to engage my young children with stories, and my children (especially those over six years) repeatedly listen to stories on CDs and Mp3s almost daily.

More Why

Through stories, I demonstrate to my children that journeys have form and meaning. Life has form and meaning. I support them to understand that Allah ﷻ shapes and plans the universe and that we drive our lives through our decisions. When I interactively tell stories, listeners can shape the characters' paths. When I read from books, they can have dialogue about what the characters do without influencing the plot. For me these processes aren't merely important for developing empathy for other people. Discussing fiction in terms of character choices gives children (and adults) safe spaces to analyse human behaviour without judging or backbiting anyone real, and to develop self-awareness of our own perspectives. I consider that to be foundational, intelligent preparation for taking responsibility for directing our life stories.

Because stories each have a beginning, middle, and end, we can identify the moments of action, dialogue, and decision-making that accumulate to a particular conclusion. Subsequently, we can become more self-aware about what stories we are creating for ourselves, and of what kinds of things we can do to change them – especially when we can draw on the mistakes and wisdom of numerous characters in various situations.

This is a world of stories. We tell ourselves stories of who we are in our inner voices. We use stories to express ourselves. We relate stories to invite people to Islam. We use stories to theorise scientific discoveries from observations. All of the messengers of Allah ﷻ told the true story of His awesome existence, and called people to believe them, to strive to return to Him, and attain His eternally blissful garden.

Sadly, we can easily limit ourselves to failure by telling ourselves that underachievement will be our story. In effect, we can make decisions and take actions to live our lives as 'tragedies', or tragic 'comedies'. Or we can strive to succeed. To be successful, we need to find solutions in contrast to trials, and keep trying, trying, trying to turn back to Allah SWT. We need to choose to live 'quests', 'rebirths', 'rags to riches', and 'overcoming the monster' plots, and 'voyage and return' stories to reach the peaceful, peaceful, peaceful garden beyond our dreams, by the grace of Allah ﷻ. Through stories, we can gain the wisdom of thousands of journeys and travels to help us – while avoiding sinful experiential knowledge and backbiting. SubhanAllah.

So, which stories will you tell? Below are some of my favourite resources to help you to include read-aloud and tell-by-heart storytelling in your Muslim home education. And you can use the 'how' section above to improvise interactive storytelling, too.

Elizabeth's favorite storytelling resources are listed on page 56 of this issue.

Interview:
Reflections from A Well-Seasoned Journey

By Chantal Blake

About ten years ago I was introduced to Roxanne, a Jamaican-American Muslim like myself who accepted Islam as an adult. Meeting at a conference in San Diego, her characteristically Californian approach to childbirth, parenting, and natural living has made her a treasured big sister figure in my life. Our annual check-ins about life, mothering and homeschooling consistently leave me motivated, affirmed, and inspired for what awaits our family around the bend. In this interview she shares what it's like to homeschool on a farm with six children, and what they've learned along the way.

Chantal Blake: When and why did your family decide to homeschool?
Roxanne: There was no clear point. My husband is a teacher and school principal. He knows the school system well and didn't want our children in it. I've been through school and hated every minute of it. I begged my mom to send me back to Jamaica because I was always an outcast, though a good student. So, for some reason, we just never planned on sending our children to school.

Chantal Blake: How has your approach to homeschooling evolved with time?
Roxanne: There's a lot of peer pressure for homeschoolers which is a sad, sad thing. For me, the pressure was memorizing Qur'an from really young and reading. I followed a Susan Wise Bauer book that was strict about how to teach reading. The child is required to sit still and not fiddle, so I started teaching my older daughter to read when she was four years old and it was horrid. It was frustrating for me and she just wanted to play. My husband asked a scholar friend about it. His advice was to do nothing. No sit-down academics and not even Qur'an until she's seven. Initially, I was resistant, but we decided to take a break.

When we first moved overseas, my daughter was six and a half. We started reading lessons again and it was so easy. She wasn't ready when we started the first time, but when she learned, there was no stopping her. So, I'm much more lax with that. I have six children--half of them read well and half don't. It's an individual thing. Fifteen years ago, I would've lost sleep but now, there's no judgement and its fine.

Chantal Blake: What have been some of the greatest challenges to your homeschooling journey?
Roxanne: Teaching multiple levels at the same time and not neglecting anybody. Everyone wants to do school, so I try to have lessons they all can understand, but also let the younger

ones sit in on lessons with older siblings whether they get it or not. I used to be fastidious about scheduling, but now I write our goals for the day in pencil and it's rare that I finish everything. If we didn't get it done that day, I erase it and move it to the next week.

Before the farm, I would plan for the school year in the summer, but now there are so many projects. I'm gardening, canning, and doing stuff outside with no time to sit. Instead, we do an agrarian school year based on the seasons. We don't really start until November when the last of the pumpkins is picked. Our school year goes longer but it works for us.

Chantal Blake: Having homeschooled in a number of countries and circumstances, what are constants in your family?
Roxanne: Flexibility. After the Susan Wise Bauer reading attempt I did Montessori for a bit, and then we fell into some aspects of Waldorf. One that I liked was morning circle time and my kids really like it too. We learn and recite poetry, memorize hadith, share things, and do some rhyming with motion for the younger kids. Even my high-schooler does it with us. We all gather together before everyone starts their individual lessons.

Chantal Blake: When you think of a successful homeschooling day, what does it entail?
Roxanne: Being able to do something with every child without frustration or emotional breakdowns. Ten years ago, getting outside would've been a daily goal that I would schedule, but now we have to go outside every day. We feed the animals first thing in the morning before we feed ourselves, milk the animals, and put the animals away in the evening. Now that we have teenagers, I don't always cook dinner. If I feel satisfied that everyone had their time and I can get out in the garden while they do their individual things, that's a really good day.

Chantal Blake: How do or will you measure the success of homeschooling in your family?
Roxanne: Years ago, college would've been the main measure as it was for me growing up. I had no choice, I had to go. But that has morphed a lot. Even with degrees, it can be hard to find work. Our goal is for all of our kids to have skills like entrepreneurship or learning a trade. Going to college is great, but it's not something we're pushing and saying that it measures whether they've succeeded or not. Love of learning is a big measure for us. We want our children to be lifelong learners and not feel that they need to depend on others for their education. We encourage them to sit with their elders to learn different skills, listen to their stories, and be of benefit to the community.

Chantal Blake: How has homeschooling changed you as an individual?
Roxanne: It has forced me to relax. You can't do things exactly how you want them done. You deal with different personalities and learning styles and realize that what works for one child may not work for another. You have to be willing to let go and move on or let go of a subject altogether and pick it up at a later time. It has also really changed my perspective on what makes a person successful in life. I no longer think it's the paper that says because you studied something for four years, you're an expert.

Roxanne's family adventures can be followed on https://www.facebook.com/Roots-n-Earth-Family-Farm-1515075755467314/.

Chapter 3
ORGANIZING AND RETHINKING THINGS

Creating An Afterschool Program For Your Child

By Iman Said

When I put an application through for a primary school place for my son earlier this year, I felt physically ill. My husband and I had been back and forth about sending him to school because we were really keen to homeschool, but circumstances had arisen that would dictate otherwise. We decided to go ahead and put an application through with the intention of withdrawing him before he began if our circumstances changed before September. They didn't.

As I labeled uniforms and other items in preparation for his first day, I felt like I had failed and my anxiety was sky-high. The first two weeks were incredibly difficult; he was adjusting to a classroom and his new routine, his sister was upset with him being away all day, and I was struggling to parent through a surge of (mostly negative) emotions.

One particularly difficult evening, I posted on Instagram asking for fine motor skills activity suggestions because he was struggling with handwriting. One response made me feel reassured and helped to calm me down considerably. It was from a homeschooling mum who I followed. She said, "My humble advice would be to not stress or panic. Observe him at his pace and go with that. Work with that pace, he will enjoy the process and before you know it, he will be writing for longer. Think of it like this – he won't be a 16 year old who can't write for ten minutes inshaAllah! So Alhamdullilah, enjoy the process bi'ithnillah." I implemented her advice and began to relax a little and realized that if I continued to be anxious about his schooling, it would transfer to him and his learning experiences. Three weeks from when she sent that message, he was whizzing through a sheet of the alphabet and could write his name completely unassisted.

I was upset at having not been able to homeschool but it dawned on me that I was only considering one way of homeschooling based on what I had seen on other people's Instagram feeds or blogs. It didn't have to be all or nothing. That is when I came across the concept of afterschooling. I jumped at the chance to create a little afterschool routine for us and it is slowly helping me come to terms with our decision.

Start Before Your Child Gets Home

Our afterschool routine begins before he is even home. One of the most important things I have had to do is ensure that more or less everything that needs to be done - housework, work, errands, and otherwise - is done before he gets home from school so that when he is home, the focus is on him as much as possible. If there are resources we need for specific activities I have planned, I gather these so we aren't wasting any time.

Traveling To Or From School Can Be A Quality Learning Time
The school day ends at 3 pm and we live two miles from school, so we walk home and that usually takes about fifteen to twenty minutes. I plan different routes back to encourage conversations. Both my children love passing building sites and looking at cranes, excavators, and bulldozers and differentiating between them. If you drive to or from school, have them listen to an audio book and discuss it, or tell them a story!

Giving Them Time To Regroup
Once we are home, my son gets changed and is straight on to his Legos, building different structures and role-playing with the policemen and robbers. He is usually low on energy at this point in the day, so I don't plan a structured activity that will overwhelm him or cause a meltdown. If I notice that he is very tired when I pick him up, I usually stop by at a little playground on our way home and running around with his sister for a little while gives him some time to perk up.

Our Afterschool Routine
A little later in the afternoon, he makes a start on homework – at the moment that is a sheet of handwriting alphabets and name writing practice - and we play a game with a phonics sound puzzle while he does this. It is then time for about half an hour of screen time when he watches "Andy's Dinosaur Adventures". He is incredibly passionate about dinosaurs and loves the series. We've made trips to the Natural History Museum in London (where the series is based out of) and he often dresses up like Andy and takes us on dinosaur adventures in our living room!

If it's a Monday, we will have been at the library for about an hour after school before going home and the children love these visits. They pick out four or five books that we then read all week, return, and start all over again.

The hour and a half before dinner is often filled with crafts, fine motor skills activities, or coloring. I created a list of fine motor skills activities, gathered all the items we need and we have a box that we pull out to work from. If the weather is favorable, we go to the park instead and take our coloring with us using pavement chalk. As they are playing with Legos or coloring, I will often play children's nasheeds or an audio book. I happened to overhear my son narrate a story as he played with some dinosaurs the other day, and I'm amazed at how much he seems to be absorbing from listening to audio books.

We also factor Arabic and Islamic studies into our afterschooling. He does attend Saturday school where they have Qur'an, Arabic, and Islamic studies, and there is homework to be completed for that too, which he enjoys doing as it involves lots of coloring and matching, as opposed to pages and pages of writing. Often on our journeys to and from school, we'll recite the surah he is learning and briefly discuss the meaning of it, drawing from our surroundings if possible.

I follow several homeschooling blogs and use lots of the resources suggested as part of our afterschooling plan. I usually have a theme for the week and try to incorporate learning with play as much as possible. For instance, we learned about why onions make your eyes tear when he was helping me peel some to make dinner.

Holiday periods are another opportunity to foster interest-led learning. Trips that we can't make during the school week can take place during half term. I recognize how important downtime is though, and will not be filling our half term or holiday periods with multiple outings and days full of structured activities.

Sometimes things don't quite go as planned and it can be a bitter pill to swallow, but if homeschooling is not a feasible choice for your family at the moment and you want to take an active and hands-on role in your child's education, there are still ways to do that and have fun with it.

Crafting The Work-Homeschool-Life Balance

By Saiyyidah Zaidi

Fitra Journal is often asked about how families can do both homeschooling and working, especially working from home, so we have turned to Certified High Performance Coach and homeschool mum Saiyyidah Zaidi.

Fitra Journal: Please give us your background, weren't you a 9-5 kind of working mum up until a few years ago?
Saiyyidah Zaidi: I had a very traditional upbringing in some ways - go to school, go to university, get a job. Well it was traditional for someone who was raised to believe that education is important. Alhamdolillah I worked very hard and was determined to do well and managed to secure a role as a director in local government were I was responsible for a budget of $500 million and regenerating schools and urban areas. I suppose you could say it was 9-5, but it was certainly many more hours than that!

Fitra Journal: What was the crux for your major lifestyle change?
Saiyyidah Zaidi: There were two factors. Firstly, I wanted more for my kids than the education system can offer and I also didn't want to put a huge amount of pressure on my kids. One of the biggest issues that we are currently experiencing is that children and young people have major mental health issues due to the pressure of grades, school workload, and lack of opportunities. The second factor is that my daughter was bullied, and the school was unable to deal with it in a way that made my daughter feel safe and secure going to school, so we took her out. That is essentially why we started to homeschool.

In terms of giving up my job to start working for myself, it is a story that is well told! [laughs] I didn't want to be complicit in some of the decisions that were being made by my colleagues in government to the point that it was affecting the wellbeing and security of young people, elderly, and other vulnerable groups. I started to become unhappy in my job and wanted out so that's what I presented to my husband.

Fitra Journal: How did your husband respond to these changes?
Saiyyidah Zaidi: MashaAllah tabarakAllah! What a great question. May Allah preserve him. He said, "Do what makes you happy". So we went from a ridiculously amazing salary to living below the basic wage! But it was okay because we were all happy even though there was a lot of

anxiety associated with the decision on my part (a lot of my friends asked me why I would give up my dream job). The interesting thing about this is that sometimes when you get close to your dream you realise it isn't something you really wanted in the first place. Profound, I know!

We had a significant change to our standard of living but it was alright as I used that opportunity to set up my own business, something I never thought I would ever do. I had never seen being a business owner or entrepreneur as an option because many business owners in my family were not that successful or had failed. It just never occurred to me that I should give it a go. And my husband has been supportive at every step alhamdolillah.

Fitra Journal: Your current family set up is a bit unconventional, even for homeschoolers, will you please explain how the work-homeschool-domestic duties are balanced in your family?
Saiyyidah Zaidi: I am not sure what a conventional homeschool family set up looks like! Ours works for us. We do homeschool and work at the same time, so we have what I call an office-classroom. We are all in the same space, the kids study independently but have us there to ask us questions. We then all 'work' together. In the afternoon or at other times of the day we can then go out and do various other activities. Our curriculum is determined by the national curriculum (English, maths, science, history, geography), Qur'an and Islamic studies, and then other skills which we think are important. For example last week we all did life-saving training and my kids know how to do CPR which could save the life of someone one day. Next week my daughter is going to a class to do silver jewelry making.

I love the flexibility that homeschooling gives and it enables us to support our kids at a time when they are very malleable. Ali ibn Abi Talib (RA) put forward a theory in which he states: "Play with them for the first seven years (of their life); then teach them for the next seven years; then advise them for the next seven years (and after that)." When you consider this in relation to homeschooling it makes you take the raising of your children more seriously.

One thing which I want to add, which is absolutely critical, is that homeschooling is not for every child, and it is not for every parent. You need to seriously consider whether it fits in with your lifestyle and also if it is the best thing for the children.

Fitra Journal: What would you say to dads who seem to think homeschooling should simply fold into a mums' other domestic duties and they remain very hands off?
Saiyyidah Zaidi: Teaching your children is a huge responsibility, it is not the same as cleaning the kitchen or cooking a meal! Not that I am saying those things aren't important but they won't leave the legacy that teaching your kids will, right? Allah made a child have two parents - mother and father - this does not mean that a father can leave all the responsibility to the mother for education. Or you can... and then you won't necessarily have raised a child that meets your high standards. So to dads out there, get involved, if you want more for your kids, get involved and raise your child(ren) together.

One interesting point, a well respected scholar once said something to me about 15 years ago and I still remember it as if he spoke to me yesterday. I know it is based on his own experience and it may not be completely true but he said that in his time of teaching children and working in dawah he had not seen one child that was raised by a single parent who was a hafidh because it takes two parents, with all the running around, the motivation, the checking in, monitoring, etc. He also said that when you have one determined parent and the support of the other, that is the best way for a young person to complete their hifz.

Take that and apply it to the rest of education as well. A family that makes the decision to homeschool needs the support of both parents. If one parent decides to homeschool and doesn't have the support of the other, chances are it will be harder and the young people involved won't benefit as much as they could.

To mums out there whose husbands are not supporting their decision to homeschool or have different goals for their children, make dua. When you make dua and you beg Allah and ask Him for help you can do anything because Allah will remove obstacles or provide the way. It is absolutely amazing to see how things unfold when you realise that Allah has your back and you look to Him for support.

Fitra Journal: Many women ask us about working from home while homeschooling. Is it possible to do both and all? What is the best approach and practices to go about this?
Saiyyidah Zaidi: It is possible to do both but you have to be very organised and have the support of the children involved. When kids are in primary age they need more engagement from the teacher so maybe that is harder to do, but then the schooling that needs to be done is just a couple of hours a day. Yes, mainstream schools teaching content can be done in a couple of hours a day if you homeschool! But you need to provide interactions for the children in other ways, and provide them with other activities, you can't just put them in front of a television or computer. If your children are older independent study is easier with some interactions from you.

So if you are interested in homeschooling and want to make it happen then create the right environment physically and mentally. Have a classroom and workspace at home. And just start! Nothing is holding you back except you. Yes, you will make mistakes, but who doesn't? It's fine, don't be too hard on yourself, take one day at a time, and just start. After a few years, you will be the one answering the questions for Fitra Journal. [Winks] And Allah knows best.

Isn't Parenting About Controlling Behaviours and Outcomes?

By Khalida Haque

The fact that children might develop an attitude, be rude and ill mannered seems to be a real concern for many parents. In the minds of a large portion of the Muslim Community it is felt that from the moment they are born children should be impeccably well behaved and never challenge or raise their voices towards their parents and their "betters". As I wrote those two sentences I found myself feeling more and more constricted. That's me - an adult. What would we imagine - and some of us may not need to imagine as we may have grown up in very restrictive environments - a child feels in such a stifling environment? We cannot expect a plant to prosper and bloom if it is being strangled at the very root.

Attitudes develop, mostly, from the attitudes that children encounter from their parents. The oft repeated phrase in parenting workshops and trainings is that "children see and children do". In trainings and therapy when exploration of controlling, coercive and strict parenting occurs, almost always, the feeling of wanting to break free and get away from this environment is described. And that feeling that a child has grown up with remains within them so that they may then get triggered in adulthood and then they may do things to escape the perceived strangulation that they are experiencing. These escapes start in childhood and can continue into adulthood. They include self harm, promiscuous and risky relationships and behaviours, thrill seeking, substance misuse, and criminal activity.

This is not to say that even with the best of parenting some children won't go off the rails. It is also useful to keep in mind that if we see attitude we will get attitude. Meaning, if we reframe what we see as attitude into something more likely, such as a child sticking to their guns, being tenacious and principled, we are likely to see the development of a child who can challenge wrongdoing and stand up against injustice.

Qur'an And Sunnah Ways of Parenting

Firstly it is essential that we clear up the common mis-thinking around the following ayah:

"And your Lord has decreed that you not worship except Him, and to parents, good treatment. Whether one or both of them reach old age [while] with you, say not to them [so much as], 'uff,' and do not repel them but speak to them a noble word." (Surah Al Isra: 23)

This verse has been used by parents against their children when they raise their voices or use foul and unseemly language with them. If a child or anyone is using such language what might help us respond better is if we contemplate the why of the use of such tone or language. Most likely it is because they are frustrated. Too often as a counsellor I see a child, now an adult, crying about how they just wanted to please their parents but they could never seem to manage it. Whatever they did, they were told it was wrong.

Imagine if you are asked to do something you don't want to do, but someone is forcing you to. They are using Qur'an and hadith to barrage you into doing their "right thing". In your heart you know it's not, so you stick to your stance and refuse. The other person does not stop. You feel that your calm, respectful, polite tone and resolving speech deteriorate into harsh, frustrated, and angry language. If you are a child and the other is an adult who is actually in the wrong here?

If we are the adult then we are the one in the wrong because as we know the child is not baligh (accountable), for them the pen is lifted. For us? Will we be encumbering ourselves with our sin as well as theirs?

A Story Of 'Umar :

A man once came to 'Umar complaining of his son's disobedience to him. 'Umar summoned the boy and spoke of his disobedience to his father and his neglect of his rights. The boy replied: "O Ameer al-Mu'mineen (Prince of believers)! Hasn't a child rights over his father?"
"Certainly", replied 'Umar.
"What are they, Ameer al-Mu'mineen?"
"That he should choose his mother, give him a good name, and teach him the Book (the Qur'an)."
"O Ameer al-Mu'mineen! My father did nothing of this. My mother was a Magian (fire worshipper). He gave me the name of Julalaan (meaning dung beetle or scarab), and he did not teach me a single letter of the Qur'an."
Turning to the father, 'Umar said: "You have come to me to complain about the disobedience of your son. You have failed in your duty to him before he has failed in his duty to you; you have done wrong to him before he has wronged you."

The previous "uff" ayah from Surah Al Isra does not tend to be used by elderly parents against their adult children. More often than not it is a child hearing it from parents who are young, fit, and healthy. What then does the ayah mean when it refers to "reach old age"? This is a misuse of Qur'an, possibly even abuse.

Mercy, Compassion And Role Modelling

We are warned against harshness in Surah Ali Imran:

"So by mercy from Allah, [O Muhammad], you were lenient with them. And if you had been rude [in speech] and harsh in heart, they would have disbanded from about you. So pardon them and ask forgiveness for them and consult them in the matter. And when you have decided, then rely upon Allah. Indeed, Allah loves those who rely [upon Him]." (Surah Ali Imran: 159)

This ayah tells us that being strict and harsh with people means that they are likely to avoid you and your company, whereas mercy and compassion brings others close to you. If this is the reaction of adults to harshness, how might a child respond to the same or similar?

Hadith Promoting Kindness And Gentleness:
"Allah is kind and He loves kindness, and He grants to those who are kind that which he does not grant to those who are severe and does not grant anything to those who use anything besides it (kindness)." *(Muslim)*

"The one who is deprived of leniency is deprived of all good." *(Muslim)*

And for the best child-parent relationships if we look at Luqman ﷺ: **"Behold,' Luqman said to his son by way of gentle advice …"** *(Surah Luqman, Ayah 13)*

And Ibrahim ﷺ and Ismail ﷺ: **"So We gave him good tidings of a forbearing boy. And when he reached with him [the age of] exertion, he said, 'O my son, indeed I have seen in a dream that I [must] sacrifice you, so see what you think.' He said, 'O my father, do as you are commanded. You will find me, if Allah wills, of the steadfast.'"** *(As Suffat: 101-102)*

Notice that the father talks to the son in endearing terms and the son, when he responds, does so in a manner similar to his father - children see, children do - in action in the Qur'an! Throughout Surah Luqman, the father continuously and consistently speaks to his son in such terms. The prophets ﷺ are the examples by which we as adults can learn. Allah made them our role models and similarly He made us examples by which our children learn. Rather than controlling, I believe that parenting is about exemplifying. Be what you want your children to be. Display the attitude, characteristics, and behaviour you want to see in them.

Finding a Blessing Where There Was Burden

By Farzana Moolla Hoosen

With the decision to homeschool, comes a plethora of doubts. *Am I doing the right thing? How will I manage? Will we be able to stick to a schedule? Will I be able to do a good job?* And with that also comes the incessant doubtful comments from the onlookers everywhere in your life. And so we keep questioning ourselves, that is until you realise, it was never about you! This opportunity to homeschool your child or children is simply a blessing from your Lord. And when you realise this, you are able to let go. Let go of the doubts, listen to your heart which is calling you to do this, and just let it be.

This is what I have learned in this short space of time that I have been blessed to homeschool. Allah has created human beings to learn, and they will learn even when they are not being taught. If you provide the correct tools, they will not only learn but learn to love to learn. And when you have achieved that love of learning, it is time to sit back and watch the seedlings germinate and develop. Simply put, watching your children learn is a miracle. As your child has learnt to walk andtalk in your care, so too can they learn to read and do mathematics within your care. In response to the question: "Are you qualified to teach your child?" I would say I was never qualified to teach them to walk and talk yet they learned to do it anyway. In the same way, they will learn to do everything else. I am merely a facilitator of their learning.

One of the greatest opportunities of having your kids at home with you during these formative years is that you can teach them to becomeAllah-conscious, and in becoming Allah-conscious they learn to become conscious of everything around them. Not only are they learning to add and subtract, read and write - they learn about the environment and how we affect it. They learn to reduce their carbon footprint by planting flowers. They learn self-sustainability by planting vegetables in their own garden patch. They learn that banana peels are not meant for the trash but can be used as fertiliser. They become confident in their ability to draw because there is no outside judgement. They learn to write and spell because they want to write their own books. The absence of being judged is an important aspect in your children developing their confidence in anything they do. As they are not confined to being like others, they can truly excel at who they are.

Amongst these immeasurable blessings, a parent becomes not only a teacher but a student - a student of life. In these years you will find yourself learning, and wanting to learn more. You will find your thirst for knowledge is insatiable. And most importantly, you will enjoy it!

"And He giveth you all that ye ask for. But if ye count the favours of Allah, never will ye be able to number them." (Qur'an: Al Kareem: 34)

The blessings of homeschooling are a mercy upon us from our Lord. May we be of those who remember to express our gratitude to our Lord, Most Merciful.

Remember you can do this and you are not alone. Before we start anything we say "Bismillah." Let this too be the way we start every day, every task of our homeschooling journey. And somewhere along the lines, you will realise that this was never about you. It was a blessing that came to be.

Chapter 4
OUR FAVOURITE RESOURCES

Foraging - An Activity To Feed The Body And Soul

By Klaudia Khan

It's harvest time here in England. Every couple of days throughout September we go to the nearby park and collect bagfuls of apples. They are delicious, juicy and full of flavor, each tree bearing a distinctive kind of fruit: some are red on the outside with crisp pink flesh, others are golden and gentle in flavour, there are big green-red apples that we prefer cooked, and there are hard red ones that I cut in sticks for snack. They taste nothing like the supermarket apples and they look different, too: big and small, bruised and marked; some would be worm-ridden, but we take care to check them and cut out any insects. There is obviously more than we can eat and because they won't keep for long we make applesauce, preserving it in jars. I like to think this is our winter stock and these few jars that we manage to fill make me really proud. They also bring keen memories of my parents' home and garden and the summers spent harvesting the fruit and vegetables grown by my father that we would pickle, marinate, or cook into jams and compotes. That was actually our winter stock of fruit in times before the supermarkets had fruit available all year round. They were good times, filled with good foods.

The trips to the park bring so much excitement for my family: my daughters love collecting apples and have learned to appreciate their natural flavour, never mind the apples' imperfections. Each has their favourite tree and for the youngest one it is hard to wait until we get back home to wash and eat the apples, she'd love to bite into them straight away. They learn a lot through the process, much more than recognizing there are edibles in the wild. Collecting apples from the park teaches them more effectively about food production than books would, and we use this time to discuss sustainability and respect for nature. But these trips also bring sadness, because there are too many apples for us to eat or even make the applesauce, and no one else seem to care, so most of the fruit ends up on the ground eaten by birds and snails or rotting away. I don't know much of the local history, but I guess this part of the park must have been an orchard once. Someone planted these trees and cared for them, they have delivered their delicious fruit for many years now. It makes me disappointed and sad that so much of natural goodness goes to waste each year.

There are other things outside in the parks we collect, too. Blackberries are plentiful around us. There is a linden tree whose blossom can be made into wonderful tea for a cold and flu remedy. There are dog roses all around us and their plump red rosehips just ask for plucking. I found a recipe for Swedish rosehip soup and I promise myself that this season I'll give it a try. We know the parks which have nice cherry trees and others with blackcurrant bushes. We know the spots where mint grows so rather than driving to the supermarket we head to the park whenever we need some.

Where I come from foraging for food in the forests and fields is a tradition and favorite summer and autumn activity. In Poland people collect mushrooms and bilberries, nuts and herbs, and obviously apples and plums from wild fruit trees growing along country roads. From my Danish friends I know that in Scandinavia they do the same. It was quite a surprise for me to learn that in the UK this practice is all but lost, and I really had to put in effort to convince my British friends to try some of nature's produce harvested in the park. It was kind of funny watching their surprise as blackberries from the hedge behind the house turned out to be as tasty as the supermarket ones. But they still remain sceptical about less known wild foods, such as blackcurrants, and they would certainly not let their kids pick anything in the park for fear of food poisoning.

I don't argue with them much, because I feel like an amateur myself. I know the most common plants and can recognize the fruits trees, but I'd love to expand my menu with wild herbs and plants that can't be found on the supermarket shelves. I've got some recipes for dandelion leaves salads and wild herb tea in my cookbooks, but I haven't yet taken the courage to try it out. Perhaps it's time to pick up my first forager's handbook and start the new wild food adventure for my family?

Kids Learn to Stitch Review and Fun Beginning Sewing Project

By Klaudia Khan

I've always thought it would be good to teach my children how to sew, at least the very basics. But then the very basic is really all I know about sewing, and to be honest I barely reach for my needle box unless there is an emergency, such as a lost button. Sewing, stitching, and embroidery may be wonderful creative outlets, and children should have a try at different activities, not necessarily being restricted to their parents' hobbies.

We needed something to motivate us and give us clear instructions on the basics. I found just the perfect book: *Kids Learn to Stitch* by Lucinda Guy and Francois Hall is a wonderfully colourful introduction to the ABCs of stitching starting with threading the needle. It has cute cartoon characters and fun, easy projects in felted wool that really appeal to my children. The difficulty level progresses slowly in the book, but it's very manageable and feels like a challenge rather than a chore.

I liked the book from its looks, and my daughters got interested in it too, so I did not have to wait long before they asked me to do some crafts from it. I suggested that they start from the beginning and I asked them to do everything by themselves – ok, I helped them thread the needle, but that's about it. They were really pleased with themselves when they completed the first project, and it was a joy to see them having fun while learning a new skill. "The Big Bad Bug" – the craft they began with – is basically a bee-shaped plush decorated with running and seed stitches to make stripes.

Next in turn was cross stitching and appliqué, and just a short introduction was enough to make them able to carry out the next project – a cute cat called "Needle Holder Nell." They felt that things were becoming tricky, but enjoyably, so then we embarked on the third project – "Pincushion Percy" – that required star stitches, simple seams, and stuffing. This is their favourite so far, but I'm sure they won't stop at that.

If you want to have a go at making Percy the mouse – or a similar creature – here are some simple instructions:

1. You need a square piece of felt in one colour plus a bit for the base and two felt circles and a long rectangle for the ears and tail in another color, also some threads, a needle, and stuffing.

2. Fold the square in half to get a triangle shape and pin the ears and the tail in place, then stitch them with cross stitch.

3. Use running stitch to make the shape of closed eyes.

4. Stitch a large star stitch on each side of the triangle for the decoration (if you like).

5. Pin the body (triangle shape) together and stitch it along one side with a simple seam; leave the bottom part open.

6. Take out the pins and stuff the mouse's body, then stitch the base to the body.

And that's it! Your pincushion mouse is ready!

Elizabeth Lymer's Favourite Storytelling Resources

Al Qur'an
The Meaning of the Holy Qur'an for Schoolchildren by Yahya Emerick

Collections of stories for storytelling
Aesop's Fables – I've mostly used the Orchard Book by Michael Morpungo
Beatrix Potter The Complete Tales by Beatrix Potter
Buddha at Bedtime by Dharmachari Nagaraja (I make minor edits to the stories)
First Stories for Thinking by Robert Fisher
* *Healing Stories for Challenging Behaviour* by Susan Perrow
Kingdom of Joy: Tales from Rumi by Abdul Rahman Azzam
Love All Creatures by M S Kayani
Rumi's Fables translated by Negar Niazi
Wise Fool: Fables from the Islamic World by Shahrukh Husain
7 Habits of Happy Kids by Sean Covey

Chapter books for engaging read-aloud
The Great Miracle: the Story of the Prophet Isa (Peace be upon him) by UK Islamic Academy
Winnie-the-Pooh: the Complete Collection of Stories and Poems by A A Milne

Audiobooks
These audios are for the family to listen to, but also for parents to learn voicework for effective storytelling: to keep your voice strong without forcing it; to break your sentences so you can breathe, vary your tone, and pause (or not) as befits the tension in the scene; to vary your spoken pace according to the pace in the content of the story; to speak with rhythm and so on.

Beatrix Potter: The Complete Tales (The unabridged stories on these six CDs are presented with a little music.)
A Gift of the Sands read by Sandy Walsh
Dawood and the Giant read by Edmund Dehn
Leyla the Sparrow read by Sandy Walsh
Nasruddin and the Donkey read by Edmund Dehn
The Ants and the Prophet read by Sandy Walsh
The Sad Camel read by Sandy Walsh
Nuh and the Great Flood read by Ramon Tikaram (These stories by Miraj Audio are available either with or without music.)

Understanding Story Structure
Seven Story Structures / Plots
http://kidcourses.com/creative-writing-kids-seven-basic-plots/
Story Arcs
http://robsanderswrites.blogspot.co.uk/2011/01/plot-and-story-arc.html

Asma Ali's Current Favorite Resources

The Usborne Write Your Own Story Book
Starting with how to plot a story, its characters, and setting, this book is a must-have for budding authors and a gem for anyone who might struggle to teach creative writing. It is packed with writing prompts and inspiration for a variety of fiction genres (including writing your own comic strip!) and kept my kids busy thinking and drafting stories with no fuss.

Mathseeds.com
Like the website says, "Maths + Fun = Mathseeds!" One of my favorite reading programs was a website called readingeggs.com so I was really excited to see that the same team of educational experts had developed another program for math - which is just as great! From kindergarten through to grade three, these lessons online follow five key characters that introduce core maths concepts in a highly engaging way. Kids then go on to complete a number of games and activities to practice what they've learned. The award system where they collect acorns at the end of lessons to spend in a virtual shop is also a lovely touch to keep children motivated.

Iman Said These Are Great Homeschool Bloggers

Pepper and Pine: https://www.pepperandpine.com/
Our Muslim Homeschool: http://ourmuslimhomeschool.com/
Jady A.: https://jadyalvarez.com/
Nurturing Nusaybah: https://www.nurturingnusaybah.com/
Raising Rayyan: http://raisingrayyaan.com/
Parenthood Muslim Style: http://parenthoodmuslimstyle.com/
Middle Way Mom: http://www.middlewaymom.com/
Sarah Javed: YouTube Channel https://www.youtube.com/channel/UCBTLXQDD2jalzGt8xwEXAPw

Homeschooling Books Written By And For Muslims
7 Steps to Start Your Muslim Homeschool: An Alternative to Traditional Schools by Jameelah Madyun
Homeschooling 101: What to expect in your first year by Abu Muawiyah Ismail Kamdar
The Muslim Family Guide to Successful Homeschooling: Advice on Teaching and Parenting the Muslim Child by Jamila Alqarnain
And, of course, *Fitra Journal* by A Global Collective Muslim Homeschoolers

For Inspiration: Klaudia Khan's Classics Reading List

English Literature:
Winnie the Pooh by A.A. Milne
Little Princess by F.H. Burnett
The Railway Children by E. Nesbit
Charlie and the Chocolate Factory by R. Dahl
The Tale of Peter Rabbit by B. Potter

Polish Literature:
Poems for Children by J. Tuwim
Poems for Children by J. Brzechwa
Clementine Loves Red by K. Boglar

European Literature:
Pippi Longstockings and The Children of Noisy Village by A. Lindgren
Moomin series by T. Jansson
Little Prince by A. de Saint-Exupery
Tales by H.C. Andersen
Eight Children and A Truck by A.C. Vestly

Pashto Literature:
Pashtun Tales by A. Ahmad
Nightingale of Peshawar – the poetry of Rahman Baba

Asian Literature:
The Arabian Nights by W. Tarnowska
The Seven Wise Princesses by W. Tarnowska
Cudowny Skarb. Tales from Uzbekistan by Z. Nowak

African Literature:
Who is King? And other tales from Africa by B. Naidoo
Greedy Zebra and other African Animal Tales by M. Hadithi

Our Contributors

Thank you, jazakAllah khairan to all the parents who have contributed their knowledge and shared their stories to *Fitra Journal*. If you have begun homeschooling, or even parenting, you know how these tasks can absorb every minute of your day. We are truly honored that you took the time for all of us.

Hafsa Abbasi is a former primary school teacher from London who now resides in Makkah. She homeschools her two young girls and runs a private nursery at home. She loves sharing her teaching tips and ideas on her social pages - Instagram and Facebook @mamateachesme and on the website www.mamateachesme.com.

Asma Ali is an avid reader, writer and dreamer who currently resides in KSA where she part-time homeschools her sons. She also writes for Little Explorers, an Islamic magazine for children.

Brooke Benoit is running her own private Sudbury-like school with her seven children on the southern coast of Morocco. She is an editor for SISTERS magazine, the founder of Fitra Journal, a writing workshop facilitator and co-host of The Big Reconnect Sleepover retreats for Muslim women (and sometimes their family members).

Chantal Blake is a writer and unschooling mom of two from New York City. She has lived abroad since 2008 and archives her stories and adventures atwww.WayfaringGreenSoul.com.

Ellie Fathie is a homeschooling mother of two from Egypt and lives in the U.K. Ellie worked as a translator and editor, and is now a trained Montessori teacher who advocates the benefits of homeschooling.

Khalida Haque is a qualified and experienced counselling psychotherapist who has a private practice, is a clinical supervisor, group facilitator, freelance writer, and counselling services manager, as well as founder and managing director of Khair khair-therapeutic.com. She is a mother of three with an on-off homeschooling tendency, having been guided by her and her children's needs.

Reyhana Ismail is a UK-based graphic designer who specializes in print design, with a primary focus on books and magazines. She has her own freelance design firm, Rey of Light, where she also creates custom-made planners and notebooks. Reyhana enjoys baking, art, and travelling with her two kids, and is also a keen swimmer.

Klaudia Khan is a Muslim mum and writer living in Yorkshire, UK. She has three homeschooled daughters and loves to learn, create and play with them.

Elizabeth Lymer is trained in storytelling and basic playwork, and has a BA in Drama (Applied). In July 2017, she adapted stories of Prophets in Palestine produced by Friends of Al-Aqsa and performed them as interactive storytelling at the Palestine Expo, London. She has worked as a creative developer for Noor Kids and Little Hibba, and has written children's rhymes and stories for Mindworks Publishing. Elizabeth has also published picture books independently via Aneesa Books. Her title Hector Hectiricty and the Missing Socks began as an interactive, improvised storytelling session with her four home educated children.

As a former lecturer in Engineering and mother of four, *Ilhaam al Maskery* developed a passion in enhancing the quality of educational experience beyond college rooms into classrooms and now - homerooms. She currently develops and facilitates enrichment workshops on a freelancing basis. She is a homeschool mom of four precious gems striving to fulfill the "Amaana" entrusted to her by Allah I and to raise a generation of Sahabas who will be the Sahabas of Prophet Muhammad in Jannah. She is inspired by the saying: "Every child deserves a teacher who never stops learning." Join her in her homeschool journey as she learns, reflects, and engages with the wider world: Instagram feeds-@inspireOM and @homeschooling_sahabas; blog- www.homeschoolingsahabas.wordpress.com)

Farzana Moolla Hoosen is from South Africa. She is a homeschooling mother of three, who has come to understand that the joy in home educating is to follow the interests of our children.

Weronika Ozpolat is a Speech and Language Therapist specialising in bilingualism. She lives in the South West of England with her Turkish Kurd husband and their three, young, homeschooled children. They are a multilingual family, speaking English and Turkish at home and learning Arabic as a third language. Weronika shares information about her multicultural family life on her blog, Multicultural Motherhood, where she writes articles about homeschooling, bilingualism and speech and language issues. Read more by Weronika on her blog: www.multiculturalmotherhood.com.

Iman Said is a working mum of two, a wife and organising junkie. She blogs over at www.andthenshesaid.com, where she shares the beautiful, chaotic, ever-changing life journey that she's on through her parenting experiences, reflections, organising and creative projects, and lots of family friendly recipes.

Saiyyidah Zaidi is a Certified High Performance Coach, Meyler Campbell trained Executive Coach, and Positive Psychologist. To find out more about how you can get results in personal and professional life go to www.Saiyyidah.com and you can start by downloading the free 'Day Planner' to enable you to set the objectives for the day and get the results you are looking for in life bi'ithnillah.

Personalise your planners and notebooks with your child's artwork!

www.reyoflightdesign.com/store

mamateachesme

- where learning at home is super fun -

Contact Hafsa for any tips and advice on homeschooling or just a chat!

Instagram: @mamateachesme Facebook: www.facebook.com/mamateachesme
website: www.mamateachesme.com

www.ingramcontent.com/pod-product-compliance
Lightning Source LLC
Chambersburg PA
CBHW070551300426
44113CB00011B/1870